Step 1: Turn it off and turn it back on again.

Did that work? If not, proceed to Step 2.

Step 2: Google it.

P.S. The following pages are for notes, doodles, to-do lists, journaling, or whatever else you want to do with the time you've saved by fixing your own IT problems.

Made in United States
North Haven, CT
03 January 2023

30580055R00114